SCHOOLING BY THE NATURAL METHOD

Schooling by
the Natural Method

by

ROLF BECHER

English edition prepared by
Major and Mrs. Patrick Maxwell

I LOWER GROSVENOR PLACE
LONDON S.W.I

This edition first published 1963

Reprinted 1972
Reprinted 1974

SBN 85131 105 9

Printed in Great Britain by
Lewis Reprints Ltd.
member of Brown Knight & Truscott Group
London and Tonbridge

I DEDICATE THIS BOOK

TO ROSWITHA KLEIN

WHO PUTS INTO PRACTICE SO

SUCCESSFULLY ALL I HAVE

TRIED TO TEACH

ACKNOWLEDGEMENT

I wish to express gratitude to Major and Mrs. Maxwell for their painstaking trouble to put my inadequate English into a proper colloquial form, and for their help in contacting a publisher for this book.

PREFACE

"There is no adequate defence, except stupidity, against the impact of a new idea." (*Percy W. Bridgman*)

I know there are already so many books about riding on your bookshelf that your first reaction may be "Good Heavens! Another book in this line!"

I understand, but I leave it to you to start thinking about riding and horses in a new way after having had a look through these pages. The ideas in this book have all been prompted by the many horses that have passed through my hands.

Associated with horses for more than thirty years in show jumping, cross country riding and hunting—not to forget the hard times of the war—I found that I had to revise a remarkable amount of dogma that has been handed on for decades among riders and instructors, without anyone stopping to ponder on it. It is so easy for one to jog away down familiar tracks, sparing the effort of thinking for oneself.

But among those riders to whom riding is more than a mere hobby—I mean people who aspire to make their hobby an art—I found many interested in the fundamental problems of horsemanship.

I do not claim that my ideas are either revolutionary or original, for both the Italian, Federico Caprilli and the German, Andreas von Flotow established and practised the ideas which are the basis of this little book.

R.B.

CONTENTS

INTRODUCTORY

BEFORE I begin these notes, let me first answer two questions I was often asked after the publication of the first edition of this book in German. These questions were "Do you axiomatically reject all dressage work?" and "What are your views on schooling?"

The first question I must answer with yes *and* no.

Yes, because I reject the rigid continental dressage as a means of training jumpers, hunters and combined training horses. The mental readiness of the horse for the task demanded in this dressage is strictly tied up with these aids. Any wandering of the horse's attention endangers performance. Good dressage of this kind therefore develops the horse's obedience, and attention to the rider, but automatically impairs the horse's initiative and the ability to look out for himself across country and over fences. Outside the riding school the horse's attention must be directed forwards to the difficulties of the going or getting over obstacles.

No, because the performance of dressage movements supples and develops the horse's muscles and every horse must be schooled to a sufficient degree of obedience. Both these requirements are most simply met by regular dressage work.

However, the paths of pure dressage and good performance across country must part eventually.

The second question I will answer in this book. As I see it there is a necessity for a training method for the cross country performer and jumper, the foundation of which is the development of the horse's initiative so that it may perform its rider's will independently. In other words, the rider sets the aim but the horse achieves its execution.

I must now stress that not every horse is capable of being trained in this way. The horse must be an easy ride, obedient and balanced. The object should be to produce a horse which could cope with a Three Day Event, and I want an elastic, relaxed and "scopey" horse. My method is based on teaching the horse through his mind. It starts in the field and progresses to the school—not the other way about.

Now don't get the idea that I am denigrating dressage—in its highest form it is horsemanship of the greatest merit. But dressage of this standard is, and should be considered to be, an end in itself.

In Germany particularly, many people hold that dressage of a high standard is the indispensable preliminary to attaining a skilled and reliable cross country horse, so many good horses are ruined before they ever leave the school.

NOTE

Fig. followed by a number refers to the Muscle Plate on page 69 and subsequent illustrations in colour. *Fig.* followed by a letter refers to illustrations in the text between pages 13 and 62.

CHAPTER ONE

The Horse's Anatomy

THIS CHAPTER does not pretend to be a veterinary text-book, but without some understanding of the mechanics of the horse's bones and muscles the reasons for much of what follows will not be clear.

THE BACK

The horse's back is a flexible bridge between shoulders and hindquarters. It provides the co-operation between hind legs and fore legs and in addition bears the weight of the rider. The controlling link is in the vertebrae, which consist of a series of flexibly connected bones. Protruding from these bones are spines, or thorn-bones of different sizes and project-ing in different directions. They slant backwards from the withers to the middle of the back at the sixteenth vertebra, where they change direction and slope forwards from there to the rump; the last five to the tail slope backwards again (*Fig. A*).

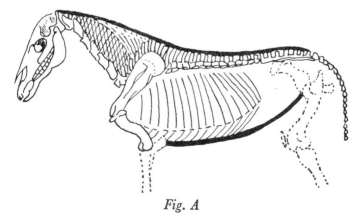

Fig. A

From the back of the skull, running over the withers and down the back, runs the CERVICAL LIGAMENT (*Fig.* 1) which joins the top of the thorn-bones together.

This ligament, anchored to head and rump, acts like the hawsers of a suspension bridge. By putting his head forward and down, the centre of the back is pulled up just as tightening the hawsers of the bridge would pull up the roadway. The wither acts as a tower or fulcrum. This, of course, is a little over-simplified, but shows that in order to round his back a horse must put his head down, and vice versa.

The muscles which operate the thorn-bones are below the ligament along the back (*Fig.* 16).

As a counterpart to the Cervical Ligament is the muscular cover of the belly, stretching from breast bone to pelvis (*Fig.* 20).

The muscle which plays the chief part in the co-ordination of movement is the LONGISSIMUS DORSI (*Fig.* 15). It runs either side of the vertebral bridge from the sacrum to the lowest (seventh) vertebra. It consists of parallel muscles running top — rear and bottom — forward. It thus joins forequarters with hind and controls contraction and extension of all paces.

It should now be plain that what is going on inside the horse's back is as important to it as the goings-on under the bonnet are to the motorist.

Now consider what happens when a heavy weight is put for the first time on a horse's back. It tries to obviate the load to begin with by tightening up all the muscles in its back and forming a hump (cold back). The muscles soon tire, and the hump subsides. The horse gets narrower above and broader below, and raises its head to relax the Cervical Ligament (*Fig.* 1). This of course merely stretches the back muscles in the opposite direction and prevents them from doing their proper job of connecting fore quarters and hind quarters in movement. Until its back is developed to take the load, no green horse can begin to move properly (*Fig. B*).

There is only one way to do this: by bringing the head forward and down, thus pulling up the back. The horse can only do this if the rider's weight is put where it can be supported to start with — immediately behind the withers, as is shown in *Fig. C*. This then allows the back muscles to relax and get on with their proper job — movement of the whole animal.

Fig. B

HIND LEGS

The hindquarters provide the forward impulsion for movement. The stifle and hock are connected by tendons (*Figs.* 25, 26) so that a forward or rearward movement of one is followed by the other. Each leg can move independently in a vertical plane from the hip downwards. The hips can move slightly, in a horizontal plane, due to the ability of the spine to twist. The large muscle (*Fig.* 22) connecting hip and stifle is always stressed whilst the horse is standing. He will rest one side or the other by putting his weight on one or the other hind leg. The large muscle beside the rump (*Fig.* 21) positions the hip joint with the back whilst the leg is being used to push the horse forward.

Fig. C

Under the back in the region of the loin are further muscles connecting back and pelvis, which help pull forward the pelvis when, for example, cantering. Around the outside (*Figs.* 23, 24) are the buttock muscles which pull the legs rearwards and are the source of power at all paces and are used for jumping.

THE FORELEGS

The forelegs are the passive partners of the hind. They serve to catch the weight as it comes forward and roll it onwards as each leg comes to the ground — as do the spokes of a wheel (*Fig. E*).

The chest of the horse hangs in a series of straps from the shoulders and elbow joints (*Fig. D*).

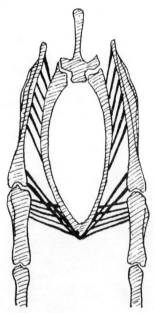

Fig. D

The LATISSIMUS DORSI (*Fig.* 17) connects the point of the shoulder to the back. Any cramping of the back affects the forelegs through this muscle by shortening and cramping the stride.

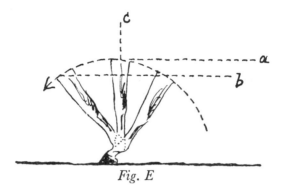

Fig. E

When the horse is standing, the FLEXORS (*Figs.* 11, 12) are equally stressed. These are the ligaments. No muscular effort is required for standing, and if, therefore, the horse rests a foreleg, lameness should be suspected.

The forelegs help little in propulsion except in going uphill and in raising the forehand when jumping. It is essential that the horse should have free forward movement of the forelegs in order to take full advantage of the push from behind, and it is therefore vital that the horse should possess sound feet and tendons. Soundness in the forelegs is maintained by progressive exercise and by discretion in what work is done at each stage of fitness.

THE NECK

The CERVICAL LIGAMENT (*Fig.* 1) runs over the withers to the head. Now we will have a look at the PORTER, which carries the head. It consists of the HEAD MUSCLE (*Fig.* 2), the LONG NECK MUSCLE (*Fig.* 5) and the WITHERS MUSCLE (*Fig.* 4).

The head muscle tires easily, which explains the difficulty and the length of time required to get the horse's head into the right position.

The divided muscle (*Fig.* 3) produces all the large movements of the horse's neck when moving or jumping. Its development, along with that of the head muscle, is of great importance. A green horse will have a triangular depression below its crest and in front of the shoulder blade and withers, which will fill out when these muscles are developed.

17

The head-neck-arm muscle (*Fig.* 6) helps lift the forelegs; if the head is raised it will cause high action with a short step in front; if lowered, a flatter, longer step. When pecking on landing over an obstacle a horse can only save himself by bringing forward a foreleg; he can only do this by stretching forward his head and neck. The head-neck-arm muscle should be allowed to remain passive and undeveloped because the horse can resist the bit by contracting this muscle (leaning on the bit).

The divided neck muscle (*Fig.* 7) however, should be well developed. It helps perform the take-off when jumping and takes the weight on landing, working through the levers of the forearm and shoulder blade. The neck end (lower) is bedded in ligaments supporting the ribs (*Fig.* 8).

The general rule should be that the top of the neck above the spine is developed and the lower part left undeveloped.

CHAPTER TWO

The Circulation and Nervous System

THE CIRCULATION of blood nourishes every part of the horse's body. Muscular effort requires large quantities of oxygen, obtained through the respiratory system. During fast work relaxation of all muscles (except those required for movement) is essential if we want to obtain the maximum performance. Excitement, fear or nervousness cut the horse's power to perform a sustained muscular effort. The psychological attitude of the animal should be considered of paramount importance during all his schooling — calmness is all.

The circulation of the blood is as follows: the left ventricle of the heart pumps clear red blood containing oxygen via branching arteries to every part of the body. The muscles contracting use the oxygen and create waste materials which then return via the veins to the right ventricle of the heart. The blood is now darker and thicker. From there it goes through the aerating and cleansing membrane of the lungs where it absorbs fresh oxygen. The reconditioned blood then goes to the left ventricle and starts its round anew.

Excitement accelerates the action of heart and lungs in preparation for the horse's natural reaction towards danger — flight. If a flat-out gallop is desired, then excitement is a good thing. The hot and excitable temperament of Thoroughbreds bred for racing is a physiological concomitant of speed. Except for short distances flat racing, however, adrenalised near-hysteria is the last thing we want. It has two evil effects, psychological, in that the horse becomes deaf to everything but its own fear, and physiological in that it cannot support the strain for long without losing condition; in other words burning up its own fat and muscle faster than its food can replace it.

For all purposes, other than sprinting, the mental attitude of flight is ruinous. Frustration of the desire to flee results in further fear and excitement, disobedience, "playing up" and so on in a vicious circle. Further, the physical results of excitement — increased blood supply, the secretion of adrenalin, faster breathing and sweating, create nervous effects such as spasmodic muscular contractions which lead to increased mental excitement. The latter takes place through the involuntary system of nerves.

The nervous system, very broadly speaking, operates like this:—

INVOLUNTARY SYSTEM

SYMPATHETIC NERVES	PARASYMPATHETIC NERVES
Control physical acceleration and mental excitement.	Control physical relaxation and mental calmness.

VOLUNTARY SYSTEM

MOTOR NERVES	SENSITIVE NERVES
Operate the muscles from the brain.	Send information from the surface of the body to the brain.

In the voluntary system are included all deliberate actions and all feelings. In the involuntary system are to be found the reflexes or automatic actions not controlled by the brain.

We can only directly affect the horse through the voluntary system. It therefore behoves us in training to get on the right side of the horse, mentally, from the very beginning. In this way the involuntary system remains dormant.

Obedience, you may say, must be enforced. Well, show me any horse who is at the top today in any field. Do you really think that the rider *forced* it to jump that six foot fence; perform that piaffe; complete that three-day event course, in obedience to his own wishes? If it were so, horsemanship would be simple — merely a matter of third-degree police methods. Obedience cannot be enforced with lasting success, but must grow gradually out of skilled training, and nervousness is the worst enemy of this training.

SOME DEFINITIONS

Having discussed the physical and nervous construction of the horse, I will now define some of the terms I am going to use later when dealing with his schooling.

Tensile Attitude

This means the attitude of the horse which allows it to be relaxed and yet ready to produce maximum power for any movement. The head should be stretched forward and down with the cervical ligament arching the back and the longissimus dorsi unburdened and free.

Thus the undeveloped horse becomes supple and his gait elastic and free. It is the foundation of the horse's education to be able to achieve this attitude at all paces, as illustrated in *Figs. P, T,* and *V* (see pages 43, 51, 61). The horse must be absolutely quiet.

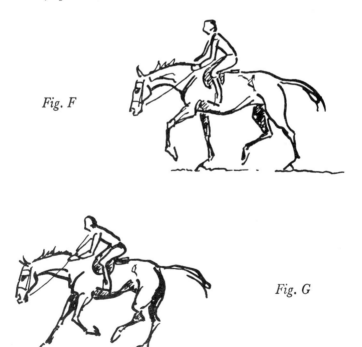

Fig. F

Fig. G

Balance

This develops out of the tensile attitude. A horse is within balance if it can travel at all paces as well without reins as it can with them, so balancing itself under the rider's weight.

This is a little more than the usual meaning of the word "balance", which refers to the distribution of weight over the four legs.

Bearing

Good bearing develops after much balanced work. The horse, having developed the right muscles, habitually uses them, naturally putting itself in the right attitudes and holding them for long periods without coercion. It cannot show real stamina across country until it reaches this stage.

Obedience to the Reins

This will be achieved by the willingness and ability of the horse to understand and obey the rider's aids. Willingness depends on mental teaching and ability depends on balance — the unbalanced horse is *unable* to obey the reins. Obedience is not obtained by compulsion or by active pulling on the reins.

CHAPTER THREE

Psychology of the Horse

MANY HORSES are unfortunately spoiled because the men who train them have the wrong outlook. The bad trainer thinks that he can teach a horse entirely through his own cleverness or skill, eventually forcing it to obey him, if not willingly then by punishment. Far too many riders possess this attitude, with the result that the horse becomes thoroughly frightened and unco-operative and is eventually rejected as useless and stupid.

Why does this happen? Usually because the rider knows what a well trained horse should *look* like, and, if he has ridden such an animal, knows also what his horse should *feel* like, *but* — he makes the fatal mistake of failing to understand that his own horse is not yet ready to learn and understand what he wishes it to do. It's brain and muscles are not yet sufficiently tuned to absorb teaching of any kind, so the rider tries to take short cuts, neglecting any relaxation, with the result that the horse becomes either frightened or "dead".

So we infer that (a) in order to get muscular co-operation the horse's brain must be tuned, and (b) the horse's will must be in co-ordination with that of his rider. How should one set about this? Firstly, be content with even the smallest measure of success attained towards getting a willing and co-operative horse which is amenable to the aids. A horse cannot be expected to learn what his rider is asking him to do in five minutes, and if he is punished for lack of understanding he will promptly become frightened, and resist the rider. In next to no time horse and rider are enemies and a useless and prolonged battle ensues. This is the reason why we see so many nappy, spoiled and unreliable horses about.

It is easy to see how the minds of a horse and his rider are attuned, particularly when jumping. A timid rider will communicate his nervousness to his mount as he approaches a

23

fence, and the horse will either refuse the obstacle, or else jump it at the last moment in a thoroughly awkward manner — particularly if it is a young and inexperienced horse.

Again, so many horses are spoiled through lack of understanding on the part of the rider: for instance, a horse jumps well over a small fence and the immediate temptation is to put him over something bigger. Up goes the fence, and the rider is immediately demanding too much of his horse at his particular stage of training. The horse refuses, or perhaps jumps the obstacle in a panic, hitting it hard. It would have been much better to pat his neck and lead him back to the stable after jumping the first small fence properly.

So, throughout the training, the accent must be on avoiding unpleasant sensations or feelings of dislike, and encouraging feelings of pleasure, thus by easy stages encouraging a horse to enjoy doing something that he would probably have rebelled against had he been shown it all at once.

Each school movement should gradually become a habit. Most habits are pleasing to the horse, and will be followed because they are acts of convenience.

When seeking information about the mentality of the horse, we must first turn to its ancestors, and the hard conditions under which they lived. The wild horse had a hard and dangerous life among other predatory animals; it possessed no arms with which to tackle its enemies, no horns and no teeth suitable for battle. Its only defence was its legs and its swiftness to carry it away from danger, and naturally all its senses were developed to a fine point. In order to give it ample warning of impending danger the sense of smell became the superior sense, supported by the quickly turning ear.

The instinctive feeling of being alone and unarmed, relying only upon his own sense of smell and hearing, led the horse to form a herd.

Although the stallion protected and kept the herd together, in times of serious trouble it was only the entire community who could offer real protection. Perhaps you will remember the well-known picture of a herd of mustangs with heads inward, pressed together to keep off attacking wolves. In this we see the final weapon of the horse. Its power of flight has come to an end and its last resort is the hoof.

As the horse has become domesticated, so its senses have adapted themselves to the new circumstances of civilisation, and it has become unfitted for a life in the wilderness. But one still has to appreciate — and it is important — that the primitive instinct is still very much alive in our present day horses. They will use their weapons if cornered; their first resort is flight.

There are numerous examples of this; a rider is trying to collect his horse by sitting well back and using sharp spurs, urging his horse to move forward against the reins. Association of ideas; discomfort — pain — danger — flight! The horse becomes more agitated, the rider harsher, the horse responds by becoming more and more frightened, and attempts to bolt. Or: the rider uses a severe bit in order to obtain more control and obedience. Association of ideas: increased pain — danger — attempted flight; with the result that the horse becomes more highly strung and nervous than ever.

There is a fundamental difference between the brain of a horse and that of a dog. This is that whereas a dog, having committed some crime, will know that trouble is impending on the return of his master, a horse possesses an automatic or reflex memory and is quite incapable of any such foreboding. The trainer must at all times bear this difference in mind when applying praise or, in rare cases, punishment.

THE SENSE OF SMELL

When going up to a horse in a stable and putting your hand through the bars of its box, you will notice that its first reaction will be to reach forward with its head and sniff the proffered hand, recognising you at once as its master, and anticipating the opening of the box door and the offering of a piece of bread from your pocket. It will come forward with full confidence, knowing that all is well. In this way you can make great strides towards gaining the confidence of your horse; it is worth remembering that a piece of bread carried in the pocket absorbs the personal smell of the man, and that bread will therefore be a far better titbit than sugar.

When training my own jumpers I have learned that I get the best results by introducing them to each new obstacle by allowing them to stand and sniff it for some time while I pat their necks and give them pieces of bread. Thus the association of ideas is pleasant, and, recognising that this new obstacle does not hurt them — in fact it is a pleasing experience associated with a reward — they are no longer suspicious.

THE EAR

A horse recognises the step of his master either with evident pleasure or (in a negative way) with fear. We all know that a murmured word will soothe and calm a horse on a lunging rein or under the saddle, and that a high, sharp call or urgent hiss will urge him to increased effort.

It is not the loudness of a certain noise that will affect the horse's reactions — rather it is the association of ideas. For example, the feed trolley of a large stable may roll upon rubber wheels but the horses will recognise it by the steps of the man pushing it along. They do not need the rattle of wheels to stir them up; rather they associate the quiet sound with their anticipation over the approaching food.

FEELING

Like men, horses feel with the entire body and as all the rider's aids are turned towards the sense of feel it may be superfluous to deal with it in this chapter. However, it is part of the theme of riding instruction, encompassing all aids of rein, leg and weight, and because all senses are linked with one another it is impossible to separate them.

SENSE OF TASTE

This is closely connected with the sense of smell and is therefore important. For instance we all know that a man with a bad cold cannot perceive a distinctive taste — an example of how closely these senses are linked.

THE EYE

The eye is not considered to be one of the most developed senses of the horse, but it is not half as bad as it is often made out to be.

Herr von Flotow, who trained horses for the 1936 Olympic Games, says that the horse is able to see almost the whole horizon due to the position of the eye. The horse sees every little movement that takes place in its immediate surroundings; it also notices the movements that take place behind the withers — for example, a slight movement of the whip — but the actual point on which the eye is focused is limited in proportion, explaining the tendency to shy at strange sights and suddenly moving objects such as flapping paper.

A horse can clearly see objects directly in front of it, but the further backward or laterally inclined the object may be, the more indistinct is his vision. His capacity of seeing in relation to the circuit is wide, but the direct gaze is low and limited; we all know that even a well trained horse when taken unexpectedly into a fence is capable at times of running out at an obstacle which it is perfectly capable of jumping properly, and this illustrates the difference between the wide capacity of *seeing generally* and *direct focus*.

Captain Caprilli's method of demonstrating the direct focus was to put his horse at a wire fence without maintaining any contact with the horse's mouth.

The eye of the horse also enables it to see extremely well in darkness, and it is well known that if the rider "can't see his hand in front of his face" he does well to abandon all attempts to steer the horse and gives him his head, in which case he will always pick his way carefully and surely home.

In nearly every case it pays to treat a horse as one would a man, but this does not apply in the case of sight because the scale of senses is different. Man is primarily a seeing creature, depending on his sight to tell him what is going on around him; he would not dream of depending on his sense of smell alone.

The horse, on the other hand, relies firstly on his sense of smell; he will not stay long enough to look at a strange object unless his nose has assured him that all is well. Naturally when he has become thoroughly used to something strange he will no longer deem it necessary to have a good sniff at it before he ventures to approach.

If the rider is to do justice to his horse he must bear carefully in mind, throughout the horse's training, that the five senses, sight, hearing, smell, taste and feel are the key to the mental life of the horse.

We must also suppose that the horse possesses some of the other senses as, for instance, the senses of locality and time. The sense of time develops only by experience, eventually becoming habit; a horse which is fed punctually every day will eventually come punctually from its paddock to be fed.

The horse's sense of locality must be distinguished from the sense of orientation in man. A man who is trying to find his way back has to bear in mind certain landmarks such as houses, trees, slopes, shrubs and so on. A horse on the other hand does not seek to find his way by the path on which he has come; he takes a direct line back to his stable or field. Therefore it seems more appropriate to say that a horse possesses a sense of locality rather than one of orientation.

INTELLIGENCE

The intelligence which a horse undoubtedly possesses develops to a large extent in this way: a reflex becomes a memory, and a memory becomes understanding. As the horse gains experience a great number of memories and ideas are knit together, and the trainer has a far reaching influence on whether the experiences gained by the horse during work accumulate essentially to positive or negative complexes. Through this we must find the key to progressive training and to absolute obedience. Every new experience gained by the horse is retained. It is either there, available at any time, or else sunk down into the subconscious.

A horse that has been spoiled through mishandling will eventually become a good horse, obedient and docile if placed in the hands of a sympathetic trainer because his instructor is able to cover the previous bad impressions by good ones. However, the initial bad experiences will soon reappear if he is again taken over by his former trainer. The horse is only capable of learning from the bottom, gradually working his way upwards. This we must bear in mind, for in the case of a spoiled horse we cannot take short cuts; we must start completely anew, for every "correction" merely leaves yet another bad impression on the horse's mind and the complications become negatively worse.

INSTINCT

The instinct holds an exceptional position and has absolutely no connection with the intelligence. It is nature's gift towards the preservation of the species and comes into action "instinctively". The instinct will, however, lead in quite the wrong direction if the essential conditions of life are altered artificially, as by civilisation.

For example, an instinctive inclination of the horse is to herd together in order to preserve the species, for he is a gregarious animal. Since man has housed his horses in stables the concept of the herd has changed to that of the stables, and in the event of a fire the excitement may induce horses that have already been rescued to break back into the blazing stable in an instinctive effort to regain the security of "the herd" — which has now been replaced by the stable. Thus the instinct leads the wrong way as the conditions of life have been artificially changed, and we see that the actual intelligence has absolutely no influence over it. Even man will, when trapped inside a blazing building, rush panic stricken to join a large crowd struggling to escape through the nearest exit even though there may be several other exits completely free — thus exhibiting behaviour contrary to reason.

The proverbial memory of the horse is well known and must not be underestimated, but it is impossible, on the other hand, to credit the horse with *reason* — a gift confined to human beings. Reason must include the capacity of abstract thought, concluding and judgment, all of which the horse is incapable. It is therefore entirely in the hands of the trainer, gifted as he is with the powers of reasoning, to develop or stunt the psychic life of his pupil.

CHAPTER FOUR

Schooling in the Open — the Terrain School

HOWEVER USEFUL the education and schooling of the horse may be within the confines of the riding school, with its walls and level ground, there are, in my opinion, many disadvantages which arise particularly during the schooling of either a young or a spoiled horse. For one thing the riding school encourages the rider to look too much at the external form, demanding an exact obedience and correctness which may well bore the horse. There is too narrow a horizon and (particularly in the covered school) a certain hot-house air which is not beneficial to horse or rider. To make a young horse fit and interested in what is going on around him, or to encourage a spoiled horse to enjoy life again, the rider must keep a draught of fresh air blowing through his own mind so to speak — and where better than out of doors?

By "terrain school" I do not necessarily mean a large open stretch of ground. A proportionately small area will do just as well for this purpose. It is always possible to find a small patch of rough ground or common with a few bushes or trees, a little grass and earth, and perhaps even some ditches or pits with a

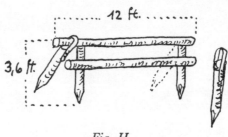

Fig. H

puddle of water in the bottom of them. This will be all that is needed; later on a few small rails here and there could probably be erected (*Fig. H*).

For the purposes of training, "cross country work" does not refer to steeplechasing, but to the methodical build up of the horse's body. From the preceding chapters it will be understood that it is of the greatest importance to develop a swinging gait with relaxed movement and supple back. Each pace *must* be held quietly and evenly — whether uphill, downhill or turning. The horse should be continually aware of the rider's aids and it will be found that horse and rider will soon learn to co-operate in order to adapt themselves to the rough terrain. To avoid any tension on the part of the horse or any tendency to hold on to the reins on the part of his rider, the rider must lean forward frequently to pat the horse's neck, low down on the shoulder with either hand. By doing this the rider is compelled to incline the upper part of the body, so getting the horse going freely into a yielding rein and thereby taking the first steps towards attaining the tensile attitude.

Naturally all this must be done at the rising trot. It is impossible for a horse to relax with a weight bumping around on his back. In the same way, the rider's seat must be easy. In cantering the knee and the inner part of the thigh become the base of the seat. To obtain the correct position for the cross country seat the rider must merely remember to keep his shoulders down, heels down, toes turned slightly outward, head up, spine straight, and hands down the sides of the neck. It will be of great help to have someone on the ground calling out these points whenever necessary.

So far as the rider is concerned the thread running through the whole foundation of schooling is that he should be able to transfer easily and pliably from one pace to another, keeping his own centre of gravity in co-ordination with that of the horse at all times, without losing his ability to apply the correct aids.

One note is necessary on the canter — when putting an untrained horse into a canter it is very necessary to watch your inner hand, being careful to allow the horse enough rein to stretch forward with a free shoulder.

As soon as the horse is going quietly and evenly at all paces, the rider may begin to ride him over logs lying on the ground. This should give rise to no difficulties if the emphasis has been on a quiet and confident approach as I have previously described. The horse must be trotted in the same quiet and balanced manner towards the log, just as if there were no obstacle in front of him. He will lower his head and neck in order to have a good look at the strange object and will then step quietly over the log or bar. Later on more logs or bars may be added, laid at different distances from each other in order to give the horse a feeling of balance and teach him to become sure footed. Whilst trotting over these logs the rider must keep his position without any interference, moving his hands forward as the horse stretches his neck, and keeping an even pressure with his calves on the horse's sides in order to keep him going steadily onwards.

Having attained the desired result we have a cool and calm horse stepping quietly over small obstacles with lengthened neck and relaxed back. This will be the basis of our training over the terrain obstacles that I have spoken about. Now these obstacles must be sufficiently rigid to present a solid appearance and yet be easily transportable and able to be quickly set up and removed. The rails themselves may be rustic and the stands furnished with iron bands so that the rails may be easily erected. By slanting the stands one may raise or lower the height of the rails. It is absolutely essential to erect these obstacles in order that they present a pleasing appearance; they should therefore

Fig. I

be flanked with shrubs or trees to form natural wings (*Fig. I*). If this is impossible a wing must be erected on whichever side of the fence is open. Remember that an island fence standing alone without wings may be a suitable obstacle to test the obedience of an experienced horse but should *never* on any account be used in schooling, as one must avoid offering the horse the slightest opportunity of running out. If this is followed from the very beginning the horse will never try to run out at a fence, simply because the thought of doing so has never occurred to him during his training. Education, conditioning and training must all be linked, and the less compulsion has been used the more successful will be the result — most particularly as far as jumping training is concerned.

Conditioning the horse is the key to successful jumping, and in the initial stages he must be jumped every day over tiny obstacles until it becomes as natural to him as walking and trotting. The whole jumping education must be permeated by calmness and cat-like suppleness — the whole thing will be spoiled by people cracking whips, shouting, and chasing horses over obstacles.

The terrain obstacles must be built up with the utmost tact. In the beginning the height should not exceed 2 ft. 6 in. to 3 ft. Take great care to avoid any excitement. An excited horse must be turned in a wide circle about six or seven yards before the jump and circled until he has again become quiet and calm. The initial jumping should always be done from the trot as it gives the horse more time to see what he is going into and lessens any tendency to rush or plunge. Double, treble and manifold obstacles will be used as the horse and rider progress, with distances between each fence of 12 yards (two canter strides); 7 yards 2 feet (one canter stride); and 4 yards (no canter stride). Naturally the distance of four yards must only be used for small fences — the height of which depends upon the degree of training reached by horse and rider.

Climbing is an excellent exercise for both horse and man. Horses are usually less afraid of climbing and sliding downhill than their riders are! It should be noted that it is essential to go down a steep slope vertically (*Fig. J*); if the horse takes an oblique track he is in severe danger of incurring a really nasty

33

c

Fig. J

fall. Climbing both downhill and uphill is an excellent back exercise for the horse, and furthers in a natural way the free use of the hock. It is as well for the rider to use a neck strap, particularly when climbing uphill, in order to avoid hampering the horse in any way with the reins.

The bank is another excellent obstacle over which to train a horse. It develops style, and should be negotiated quietly and evenly at all paces. Later on one can combine all manner of obstacles with the bank; poles before, on top, and behind — all of which improve the style and further the horse's skill at jumping. The great value of the bank and of all bank combinations is the compulsory arching of the horse's back to give a rounded jump (*Fig. K*).

Fig. K

Whether working with or without obstacles in the terrain school the general outline of the foundation schooling will be the same. When two or more horses are being trained in the school at the same time it is at first practical to set them "following my leader" in all directions, but eventually each one should become used to taking his own line. Particularly when jumping a young and apprehensive horse or a spoiled one, it is just as well to follow on behind a skilled jumper in order to instil confidence.

It is always necessary to regulate pace and over-exuberance to a certain extent, but this must be done with the minimum of rein aid; out of this will develop control of balance, but aids with the minimum rein application will only be successful if applied from a pliable seat position, driving the horse into a turn against the outside rein in order to make him stretch down and forward to it.

Working in this way you will seldom need to punish the horse — but don't forget to carry that piece of bread in your pocket as a reward!

If a free lane is available it may be used to limber the horse up, particularly after a rest day. I will go into further use of the free lane in a later chapter.

It is impossible to build a better foundation for horse and rider than in the terrain school; the value of exercises over uneven terrain is found in the resulting control of balance which in my opinion is not to be attained elsewhere.

CHAPTER FIVE

Fundamental School Work

RELAXED MOVEMENT, COLLECTION, TENSION, BALANCE

The ultimate object of training and work in the school is a skilled performance from the horse in the open air.

Let me first condense everything I have mentioned:

(a) Training must never be based on compulsion because it would lead to resistance and muscular spasms.

(b) All training must be built up on relaxed movements of the horse.

(c) A horse is relaxed when using its muscles with power and energy, both willingly and without any spasmodic movement.

(d) That is to say, with harmonious and elastic gaits, the outward signs of which are: head and neck stretching out and down towards a yielding rein; all paces held evenly with smooth action; tail carried gaily, and willing obedience to gentle aids.

When one has attained relaxed and free movement, it is time to start teaching the horse the beginnings of collection. By forming our sound foundation in the terrain school we have established the basis of collection in driving the horse forward into the reins, in the maintenance of steady even paces at all times, and in the catching up and balancing of the horse whilst riding him into turns and changing from a fast to a slower pace.

The general idea of collection may be defined as "pulling the horse together"; this can only be done if both horse and rider are relaxed, for any tension will resist collection.

The foundation of collection is based on the rider's legs urging the horse to take more active strides, his hand ready to regulate the pace without shortening and cramping the neck.

In the case of the advanced school horse ridden with increased collection, the rider's legs are urging the horse even more strongly into the reins whilst his hands are leading the swing backwards to increased engagement of the hocks. Increased collection should not be attempted until the rider is able to sit down comfortably in the saddle without any bumping and with the horse showing no unevenness of stride or sign of tension. The idea of "relaxed movement" must be an organic flexion and extension of the muscles. The horse is using its muscles in accordance with the effort required in the same way as an athlete strains every muscle and nerve for the task in hand. Such tension, however, must be founded on relaxation, for any useless tension will spoil a good performance, and it is exactly the same with a horse — every unnecessary tension is wrong.

Tension will appear if the rider lacks patience or thinks that he can achieve the desired result by pulling the neck into position with the reins and forcing the hind legs forward by means of strong leg aids without first having achieved a supple and elastic back. It is often forgotten that correct head carriage originates in the tensile attitude, from which we can discern the point at which the carriage becomes either a correct collection or else a spasmodic tension, which must at all costs be avoided.

Now let us look at the anatomical co-ordination in order to understand the correct transition from the tensile attitude (basic foundation) to the relative attitude — the next rung of the ladder.

By means of the tensile attitude the cervical ligament raised the thorn bones of the back vertebrae, arching the back. Thus the longissimus dorsi became free from the weight to a large extent, and could develop and become strong.

By means of the opposite attitude however, the longissimus dorsi is obliged to carry the weight. Tightened by the increased activity of the hind legs the fibres of this muscle are closing up together, stretching from behind-above to before-below.

The longissimus dorsi is doing in reverse with the head and neck what the cervical ligament was doing with the thorn bones, namely raising them and forming the nucleus of the relative attitude. It is also holding the ribs and belly muscles, and flexing and extending the oblique back muscle, thus completing a system of a closed muscle ring.

From this we can see that it is only possible to get a harmonic co-operation of the whole organism if all muscles are working correctly; one must never attempt to develop a specific muscle without a build up of the whole body. Fidgety horses will always produce uneven paces, as mental excitement will produce bodily tension. The horse will take enormous strides with head and tail raised high because the whole muscular ring is in a spasm, and a horse schooled in this way will not only fail to produce maximum efficiency — he will be an abomination to sit upon! His concave back is produced by the bumping seat and heavy hands of the rider; the suppleness of the back is spoiled completely, and the lower part of his neck shows strong muscular development which should not be present. Two opposing forces are clashing, ruining the horse in body and mind (*Fig. L*). Such a horse throws his legs out haphazardly — the hoof does not come to the ground on the point at which it was aimed; rather it appears to fall from the heavens!

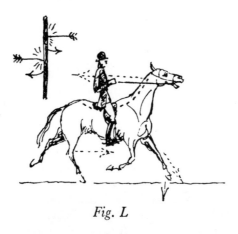

Fig. L

Now let us try to understand the moment at which the horse becomes correctly balanced. It is at the very moment when the rider's centre of gravity comes into unison with that of the horse. I will explain this by three examples (*Fig. M*).

Horse in motion:—The swing coming from the hind quarter and the forward movement brings the centre of gravity far forward. The rider has to incline his body in order to remain balanced.

Horse standing:—The centre of gravity approaches the middle; no movement takes place and the rider's seat is erect.

High school horse:—The centre of gravity approaches the hind quarter. The upper part of the rider's body is inclined backwards in order to join the centre of gravity.

Fig. M

We may compare a well prepared horse with a pair of scales which have to be continually balanced through delicate application of the aids (*Fig. N*). Every weight put into the scale behind by the driving aids has to tally with the weight in the front scale by the rein aids if the scale is not to tilt unevenly in either direction.

(Example a.) The rider is driving the horse on (weight put into the back scale) so the horse must hold the weight in the front scale.

(Example b.) The rider is checking the pace (weight put into the front scale) so the horse has to get his hind legs under him (weight into the scale behind).

The centre of motion in this balance is the rider's spine; it is therefore also the centre of all aids.

Fig. N

Naturally there will be setbacks in the schooling of every horse due to the unaccustomed use of muscles which may cause temporary stiffness or pain. Under such circumstances it would be a grave mistake to try to force the horse to carry out a particular movement because it is essential for the horse to remain willing and obedient, which, of course, he cannot do if every muscle in his body is aching! For instance one cannot expect a horse to execute a very small circle until such time as his muscles are tuned up and he himself is fit.

As the skilled school rider of classic style works through the collected attitude, leading the swing of the hind quarter back through the reins, so the terrain rider works with the natural carriage of the horse which has grown up out of the tensile attitude. Making his horse supple and pleasing to ride through balancing exercises and nimbleness of foot, he takes care that the horse remains balanced in every situation. A turn ridden into a corner but not out of it permits a minimum amount of rein aids because the wall of the school naturally limits the turn. The horse himself must bend his back to complete the turn in order to keep his balance. Such an exercise will encourage obedience to weight and leg aids. The natural collection effected by the turn remains, without the necessity of checking with the reins.

As the horse's education progresses the carriage of the horse will eventually appear so striking that it will be possible to ride turns in the open, without the confinement of a wall, with complete equilibrium and a minimum of checking aids.

I do not mean that the cross country rider should renounce all use of rein aids, by any means, for the cross country horse must willingly accept the reins; it must also accept and obey all checking aids, but at the same time it must be capable of remaining in each pace over any going, still retaining balance, with the reins slack on its neck. For if the horse is to be entirely reliable across country it must never be in any way *dependent* upon the reins.

We must remember that the horse is never obliged to accommodate himself to his rider, but that the rider must learn to accommodate himself to each horse. It is up to him to use the exercises correctly, with a suitable balance of the aids, using his understanding of the horse's mentality — for every horse is different and no two horses can be trained according to a set pattern or schedule. The rider's tact and understanding will be the key to producing a successful horse — and there we must draw the line between handicraft and true art.

CHAPTER SIX

The Forward Seat

THE IDEA of the forward seat is often misunderstood because the function of the different angles of the body are not clearly described. As soon as the angles do not appear to fit one another the whole seat becomes inefficient, so let us have a look at *Figs. O* and *P* in order to see the inherent possibilities of both the dressage and the forward seats.

Fig. O

DRESSAGE SEAT: The rider is sitting upright in the centre of the saddle. The rider's loin (pelvis, sacrum) works directly in contact with the horse's back, and is the centre of all driving and checking aids. The rider's legs are used only to tell the horse what to do. Thus the supporting structure, foundation and base, will be the rider's posterior.

FORWARD SEAT: The stirrups will be four to six holes shorter than in dressage work. The angle of the hip and knee alter, becoming more acute, and the rider's posterior becomes ineffectual. The base of the seat now becomes the rider's knee —leg— foot.

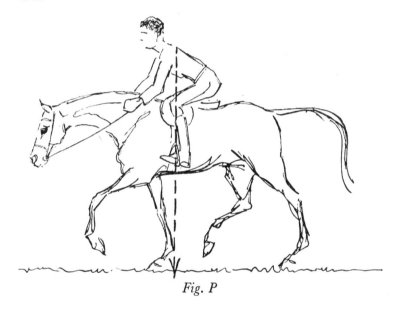

Fig. P

The centre of gravity, which is so important to maintain, lies in the perpendicular line of the stirrup leather. In order to maintain this position it is necessary to shift the rider's body as follows: the moment he starts trotting or cantering he must shift his knee some inches back in the saddle, because the knee must be near the centre of gravity, which is near the stirrup leather. The thigh will automatically shift backwards, bringing the buttocks back into the correct place.

43

If the rider were to try to keep his upright seat he would be well behind the centre of gravity; therefore he must incline the upper part of the body forward (out of the original hip angle) in order to balance his body. By doing this he will find that he has adopted the perfect line through shoulder — knee — foot. Now, with hands lowered down the side of the horse's neck he represents the perfect forward seat. The base is correct (knee — leg — foot); he is exactly on the centre of gravity, and from this perfect base he is able to drive as well as to check his horse. Again we may say that "From the base all aids come forth, and to the base all aids return".

Strict attention must be paid to attaining the correct position. Any deviation from this position, for instance a "turned over" or "head over heels" appearance is quite wrong as it is in front of the centre of gravity. These common errors can only be noticed by watching the base of knee — leg — foot; never by watching the upper part of the rider's body. For example, it is quite permissible for the rider's shoulder to reach down practically to the horse's wither without the rider being over the centre of gravity, but ONLY if his base maintains the original position (*Fig. Q*), for as soon as foot or heel deviate from their position and move far behind the girth the rider is immediately in the "head over heels" position, and the angles no longer "fit". This is of paramount importance.

Fig. Q

a) Base out of place. Rider top heavy, legs ineffective.

b) The same rider correct, base in order, shoulders down, giving hands, legs all right.

44

In order to obtain a perfect base it is necessary to put the feet "home" in the irons; when riding in the dressage position the feet should never be home in the stirrup because it would interfere with elasticity. So remember that there are two bases; firstly the base of which the rider's posterior forms the foundation, and secondly the base with the foundation of knee, leg and foot. The dressage rider is dependent on the power of his seat and loins to obtain results, whereas the jumping rider is not.

In considering the whole idea of balance one must beware of mixing static with dynamic facts. A ski jumper flying through the air will be quite out of the centre of gravity from a static viewpoint but perfectly within it from a dynamic point of view. Imagine a bear rolling across a stage on a large ball. He must strive to keep his centre of gravity all the time, because if he puts too much weight on his hind paws the ball will roll out in front of him and if he puts too much weight on his front paws the ball rolls out behind him, turning him head over heels. If, on the other hand, he maintains perfect balance, he is able to keep his ball rolling evenly, to speed it up or slow it down at will. This is the key to a perfect forward seat — dynamic as opposed to static balance.

A well taught rider must be able from the forward seat to get his horse in front of his legs into the jump — going unwaveringly forward in case of an impending refusal. If he is unable to do this, his education has been at fault. Perfection will only be attained when the whole performance appears as childs play to the spectator; but never forget that the core of the forward seat is the forward impulse!

CHAPTER SEVEN

Riding Over Obstacles and Jumping

THE GOOD jumper develops out of the foundation built up in the terrain school. This foundation has produced enough suppleness and power to make a further building up of jumping ability a simple task, for riding over obstacles becomes jumping only by virtue of higher measurements, and the confidence needed to take an obstacle within its stride has been instilled in the horse by going from easy to more difficult tasks in the terrain school. It is at this point especially that we must appreciate the individuality of each horse. It is brought home to us that no two horses can be treated alike and the delicate touch of the trainer becomes a cardinal point.

The difficulty of a higher jump lies in finding the correct point of take-off, so it is most important to teach the horse to gauge his distances correctly (*Fig. R*).

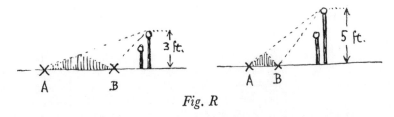

Fig. R

The judging of the take-off is not as difficult over a low fence as it is over a high one. A horse jumping an obstacle of three feet in height will overcome any difficulty by taking off somewhere between points A and B. It is exactly the same over a fence of five feet high, but here the horse has to measure his canter strides far more precisely in order to take-off between these limits. When a man about to jump an obstacle fails to find his point of take-off, his natural instinct is not to jump. It is exactly the same with a horse; if at first the horse makes this mistake and refuses to take-off we must understand that it is not necessarily a disobedience but more probably common sense — at any rate he has better reason for stopping than the rider on his back has for administering punishment! Every rider must learn to distinguish precisely between disobedience, misunderstanding or misfortune!

It is not difficult to teach the horse to gauge his distance methodically; we know that the measurement of each canter stride is roughly four yards and all we need do is place a cavaletti in front of the jump in order that the horse should be right for his fence. The cavaletti should be placed either eight or twelve yards in front of the fence, and from this exercise it will soon be found that the horse gets the feeling of distance and quickly learns to divide it up into canter strides. Later on the rider will have to appreciate that a high straight fence is far more difficult to gauge than a slanted obstacle such as a triple bar, but it is no good starting with difficult tasks; far better to let the horse develop his skill over easy fences. Let me repeat that all jumps *must* be furnished with wings as I have previously explained, so that it will never occur to the horse to run out.

If you have a loose lane available it will be very useful for jumping education. An improvised lane may always be erected by putting up laths on tripods round the edge of a riding school.

When loose laning a horse, the instructor must stand in the middle of the school with about three helpers, a feed tin of oats and a few pieces of bread or carrot. The horse is then led into the arena without saddle or bridle and turned loose. He is then allowed to do as he likes; walk around sniffing at things, looking about him, or perhaps even rolling — a sure sign of relaxation. When he appears to be quite confident he is led on to the track with a groom or helper on each side of the lane in order to drive him on by means of a short stick held in the outstretched hand. When the horse has completed a few rounds the drawled order "T-u-r-n" may be given, and he will be sent round in the opposite direction. When he has finished he will be halted by the order "H-a-l-t" and encouraged to come into the middle of the school to receive his reward. After this he must be led quietly out of the arena and the next horse may be led in. All cracking of the whip and useless shouting must be avoided.

The initial obstacles should be low, raised gradually as the horse develops skill. Then double or manifold obstacles may be used at distances of four, eight or twelve yards apart. Such loose lane jumping must be treated as an exercise to develop the confidence of the horse. Every movement must be carried out with calmness and built up logically. Any excitement or hastiness in the trainer will be communicated to the horse and spoil the education. Loose laning also encourages the horse to adopt a ducking movement before his fence — lowering the head and neck as he approaches the obstacle.

THE RIDER

When approaching a fence the rider must hold the horse closely with his legs, lowering the heel and knee. His shoulders and hands must yield to the rein, moving forward and downward to avoid a sudden jerk at the horse's mouth in the case of a premature take-off. Throughout the actual leap (take-off, in the air and landing) the rider's shoulders must remain forward. His hands must move with the horse — forward and down along the neck. Consequently his seat will lift slightly out of the saddle, but the rider must not try to lift himself by standing in his stirrups because this would restrict the effective jumping seat. Ideally the rider should maintain gentle contact with the horse's mouth throughout, but it is far better to abandon all attempts to maintain this contact rather than check the freedom of the horse with a short, severe rein, for the most damage caused as far as jumping is concerned is through the bad hands of the rider. Tweaking the horse's mouth before the jump is a widespread evil which has its roots in the mistaken idea that the rider must show his horse where to take-off; it can easily amount to what is almost a nervous mania. A horse that has been subjected to such tweaking loses all self confidence and feeling of security. He no longer has faith in gauging the take-off for himself and I can only say that in order to correct such a horse (or rider) it will be necessary to remove the reins or fasten them round his neck in such a way that there is absolutely no contact with his mouth, and with patience he will overcome this defect.

All natural furnishings of the terrain such as walls, banks, ditches, hedges, etc., should be eventually combined with rails and incorporated into the jumping training, for the more different obstacles a horse is used to jumping, the more skilled he will become. It is useless to go on jumping over a single rail stuck into the wall of the school day after day — the horse will merely become thoroughly bored.

Every leap must be a rhythmic movement fitted into an arc. As I have said before, the use of banks and bank combinations is an excellent way of developing correct style when jumping.

There are several ways in which we can make the best use of cavalettis and fences in order to improve defective style of jumping in the horse. Let us look at the following examples (*Fig. S*).

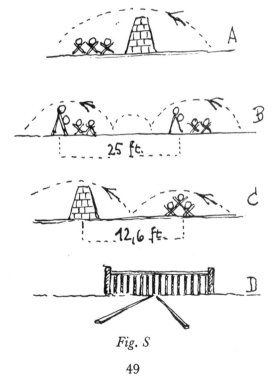

Fig. S

49

A. Cavalettis placed behind the obstacle force a horse which jumps with hollowed back and head in the air to stretch his head, neck and back, because he catches sight of them in mid-air and must necessarily lower his head and neck in order to get over them.

B and C. Cavalettis placed in front of the jump will correct a horse which is bad at judging his distances through dividing his canter strides wrongly and getting under the fence. The cavaletti should of course be placed four, eight or twelve yards in front of the fence as I have already described.

D. Two poles laid at an angle flat in front of the jump to form an inverted V, the point of which meets the middle of the fence's ground line as viewed from the take-off side, will make a horse that gets under his fences stand back instead.

Never forget to conduct all jumping schooling in a pleasant and vivacious manner in order to foster the mental and bodily swing. The horse needs a powerful back and hind quarter for jumping and this is exactly the end to which all our training has been directed. Do not forget to do a certain amount of jumping from the trot, for by jumping out of the trot the muscles of the back and hind quarter become exceedingly well developed. So the horse becomes physically strong and muscular which leads to self confidence and efficiency; trusting in its own power and judgment it will never refuse an obstacle unless something goes drastically wrong. Also a horse which is used to jumping from a trot will take an obstacle at the canter very easily because it can make even better use of the swing of this gait. Successive training of horses by trotting over jumps, first on the lunging rein and then either free or under the saddle brings on the actual jumping very quickly and pays dividends when he is asked to jump from the canter. In my opinion it is impossible to reschool a spoiled or excitable horse without resorting to this jumping from the trot.

THE TROTTING LANE

Exercise over cavalettis

The purpose of cavaletti work is to attain the tensile attitude and control of balance by getting a swinging back. This particular exercise may either be of use or damaging, for we must realise that to extract any value from this exercise the horse must trot freely over the cavalettis with downward stretched nose and swinging back as in *Fig. T.*

Fig. T

It will be damaging if the horse is permitted to strain his back by stepping high over the rails with a hackney knee action as in *Fig. U.* The normal distance apart of cavalettis used for the trotting lane is about four feet six inches to five feet. When an increased tensile attitude has been achieved the distance can be increased to six feet. The height of each cavaletti should not exceed eight inches for trotting work, lest the horse should start to stiffen his back and produce undesirable knee action. For canter work, however, the cavaletti should be higher and placed

Fig. U

51

at distances of four, eight or twelve yards apart. The cavaletti itself should consist of a rail about five to six inches in diameter supported at each end by crossed logs. The rails should not be shorter than eight feet in length because the rider would then have to hold the horse into them by means of the reins; this would spoil the exercise, the whole point of which is that the horse should learn to find its own balance without rein aids.

In order to maintain a free swing of the horse's body the rider must hold the forward seat with low shoulders and low, gentle hands, avoiding all bumping and gliding into every movement through a firm knee position with heels down and toes turned slightly out. The rider should be in the same position as that used in trotting downhill.

The position of the cavalettis prescribes where and how the horse shall place his feet, drawing its attention to the terrain, which is the other reason why the rider should not apply any rein aids in this exercise — otherwise the exercise will merely be a waste of time.

The rider's back muscles will at first be under immense strain during this exercise, for he has to keep the upper part of his body within the centre of gravity without any support from the rein.

Chasing the horse over these cavalettis must be strictly avoided because it would spoil the improvement and furtherance of natural balance.

The cavalettis may also be laid like beams, suitable for work on the lunge. It may be difficult at first for the horse to maintain balance whilst turning, but this will soon come with practice. The skilled horse and rider may use the cavalettis in a serpentine down the long side of the school, in a square, or in a figure eight, all of which are good exercises for teaching the horse to respond quickly to all weight aids.

In cantering over cavalettis it will be observed that the horse has to put his hind feet side by side in the moment of taking-off between each, instead of one in front of the other as he would do in ordinary canter schooling; this is the position necessary for jumping and the horse learns the easy way to take-off.

It is of great instructional value to the horse if the exercise with cavalettis can be combined with that of jumping. For example, if four or five trotting cavalettis are laid in front of a little obstacle or small double at a distance of four yards, the horse first has to balance himself in order to negotiate the cavalettis, and afterwards to pass straight into the jumping movements proper.

Psychologically the cavaletti exercises make the horse independent. Work with cavalettis is the foundation of working over fences and directs the horse's attention to the going that lies ahead and to the obstacles. On the other hand, the work in the school is directed strictly backwards to the rider's aids.

CHAPTER EIGHT

Correction of the Spoiled Horse

HAVING READ the preceding chapters the reader will now know where to look in order to find the root of the trouble. In every case the trouble is partly caused through previous mishandling, and the first step towards corrective training is relaxation. Go back to the beginning and instil confidence and complete freedom from muscular spasms in the animal, training him from scratch as you would a young remount.

The basic difference between teaching a young horse and reschooling a spoiled one is that whereas the young horse is merely to be taught step by step along the right lines, the spoiled horse must first learn to forget his wrong ideas before we can begin to build up his training.

This will be a long and arduous task, for the rider must learn to understand what is going through the horse's mind, his likes and dislikes, whilst the horse, who has learned to be thoroughly unco-operative, turns all his mental and physical resources towards fighting and resisting every step. Our initial task must therefore be to try and discover exactly what mistakes his former rider has made, so that we may gradually convert his feelings of dislike into pleasant sensations. The likes and dislikes of the horse will again prove that the "psychological moment" is the basis of all education and schooling, and that each battle between horse and rider can only delay success.

Bearing in mind the anatomical considerations which I have already pointed out, progress in training will depend to a great extent on the muscular development. Every intense muscular effort which will cause pain and fright must be avoided, as this would lead to resistance.

CONDITIONING

Bearing in mind the great importance of muscular development and fitness it will be most beneficial, especially in the case of a young horse, to give him daily periods of quiet, free trotting and cantering, endeavouring at all times to maintain the tensile attitude. Exercises with cavalettis and work over rails and banks also develop muscle and stamina.

If the rider works only within the boundaries of the school he is tempted to attach far too much importance to external attitudes such as collection. The horse will become bored; he cannot understand the demands made of him, so why should he carry out an apparently pointless movement again and again? But travelling across country, uphill and downhill, across all kinds of terrain, the horse is forced to collect and balance himself, not by his rider, but by his environment. He will achieve natural balance and collection without knowing that he is doing so, thereby developing all the muscles that we wish him to.

Now let us look at the spoiled horse. Usually such an animal has been overschooled. His rider has probably neglected the psychological approach in his training and relied upon compulsion as the means to an end. So the horse's mind remains undeveloped; his intelligence has never been put to task, for he has blindly tried to obey his rider, resulting in a profound misunderstanding. In such a case we may seem to achieve little or no success through cross country work, but, at the same time, in order to correct him we must take him out into the open so that he can learn to forget the aids which he has come to regard as painful and unpleasant. He must learn gradually to obey the aids; over rough country he will have to obey them through sheer necessity if he is to move at all.

All exercises with this horse must be carried out in such a way that he does not realise that he is obeying anything but his own natural instincts.

It would be as useless to set out a pattern for schooling horses as it would be to set out a pattern of behaviour for all men. The point is that the trainer is an individual with his own personality and animals possess an infallible instinct as to whom they can trust. It is personality as much as skill that breeds confidence in the horse; if he can feel that his trainer is quietly confident he will not become nervous or excitable himself.

Horses that have become really nervous and have lost all

55

confidence in man must undergo a thorough course of calming work before we can start even basic schooling. The horse may be taken into a riding school without saddle or bridle and allowed to do as he pleases with the trainer standing nearby, quite still, with pieces of bread or carrot to hand. Eventually he will sniff at strange obstacles without the slightest sign of fear or excitement and perhaps even roll — a certain sign that he feels at ease. Later on, when his confidence is beginning to return he may be led by the trainer in hand over small obstacles, between poles and so on.

When the calming work has reached this stage, the trainer may start riding him over small obstacles, applying the forward seat without any contact with the horse's mouth. At this stage the horse must hardly realise that there is a rider on his back. Gradually the trainer must start employing first aids of weight, and then leg aids. Positive rein aids must not be used yet.

When the horse is at last responding willingly to weight and leg aids (the rider now maintaining light contact with the mouth), jumping freely and quietly with natural balance over small obstacles and cavalettis, we can at length consider the corrective training to be finished and can start on the basic schooling.

If we define instinct as an innate impulse leading to a suitable action without thought or knowledge, it is easy to understand that many horses are spoiled because their feelings of dislike have been challenged. It is certain that horses possess far more than mere instinct; they undoubtedly possess intelligence, and it follows that as a result of lasting wrong education a chain of bad habits will appear. Every rider (consciously or unconsciously) works through the horse's instinct by adding to it either positive or negative complexes. Although education and training of all horses points finally to the same aim, it is far easier to work with young horses than with spoiled ones, because the young horse views its trainer with no preconceived notions or aversions whilst a spoiled horse must first be rid of all negative complexes before the foundation of a sound training can be laid. Remember that a horse will never learn otherwise than anew because its mind is not able to infer or to recognise cause and effect by thinking.

CHAPTER NINE

Subsidiary Reins

EVERYONE WHO has attempted to correct a spoiled horse knows only too well how difficult it is to get the horse concerned going trustfully into his bit. In fact there are very few horses indeed which really accept the bit; this we must bear in mind when attempting corrective training.

The reason for this common defect in training is usually too much use of the reins with over-active hands. Naturally the animal offers resistance against this, and the outward signs are: a spasmodic back muscle system, a strained muscular system below the cervical vertebrae column — in which all the rider's aids come to a full stop — a hard part of the parotid gland, an open mouth and a swishing tail. If the rider tries to overcome this by roughly urging the horse forward the result is an immediate worsening of all these reactions. The horse strains at the throat and becomes fidgety; the rider pulls harder on his reins and by such systematic throttling of the windpipe produces shortness of breath, followed by fear, and culminating in violent resistance.

It is most important that the rider should learn to recognise the difference in feeling between a horse that is truly "on the bit" and one that is "behind" or "over" the bit. If he is absolutely certain how the horse should feel on the end of the reins he has at his disposal a wonderful remedy which will induce the horse to adopt a relaxed gait and tensile attitude; let me call this remedy a LOOP REIN or RUNNING REIN.

With this rein it is possible to get a spoiled horse, which has hitherto been straining and shortening its neck in resistance, into the correct tensile attitude within a relatively short space of time. As I have previously pointed out, this depends upon removal of muscular strain below the cervical vertebrae column. By this I do not mean that all our attention must be confined to the neck, but the one is linked with the other; for example if the horse stretches its neck the back automatically arches, and merely by watching we will see that the horse will then accept driving aids without resistance in the back and neck.

The concave horse must become a convex one. This means a complete change of the whole muscular attitude of the horse. We must quickly learn to recognise any sign of muscular strain, modify the training if necessary and proceed in an understanding and patient manner.

I have used with great success a running rein (each rein eight feet long) which I buckle to the girth below and between the forelegs, running upwards from inside the outside through the snaffle rings. When mounted, the rider must not apply this rein alone, but use it together with an ordinary snaffle rein. When working on the lunge the running rein alone may be used. It is vital to yield with the running rein immediately the horse becomes compliant; it would be of little use to explain this in more detail because it is entirely a matter of sensitivity of feeling, and those riders who cannot feel immediately the horse responds should on no account use this rein.

The running rein to the horse is Ariadne's thread leading out of the labyrinth of his rider's misunderstood aids. Sliding down the rein to the bit the horse finds its way to the tensile attitude, to relaxed gaits and to a pliable foundation. When working with the running rein the rider must only apply one side of the rein at a time — simultaneous application of both reins would lead to an incorrect influence of the muscles. The running rein is a remedy to settle the horse's neck on its base, to bend the neck and to limit its upward movement, but it must *never* be used as a block and pulley downwards!

There are trainers who dislike and condemn the use of the running rein on the grounds that to be effective it must be pulled backwards, which of course is not so, and anyone who has used the running rein properly and understood its use will always stick to it for the horse's sake.

Another subsidiary rein I should like to mention is the RUNNING MARTINGALE. Contrary to the running rein, the martingale is not a rein with which to correct the horse. You may use it on a horse which you have not had the opportunity to school as it mitigates every jerk caused by the rider's hands, and offers a useful prop by its neck strap when riding across country — especially when climbing uphill. Essentially the running martingale is a rein for the rider and not for the horse. Buckled too short it is harmful, for every horse resists reining back or down by force and becomes fidgety. This martingale is adjusted correctly if the snaffle rein shows an even line between the snaffle ring and the rider's hand.

The STANDING MARTINGALE is not suitable for jumping. It works in a rigid manner and impairs the freedom of the head and neck. It is, however, a very suitable subsidiary rein to use when teaching beginners who are unable to make their horses go in proper formation.

Concerning bits, I like the flexible RUBBER SNAFFLE best for jumping. All well trained horses are easy to manage in it and spoiled horses regain confidence in the reins and in the rider's hands.

The curb bit is, in my opinion, only a bit for the well educated school horse and rider. It causes immense damage in inexperienced hands and it is utter nonsense to rig up a horse in a curb bit in order to prevent its bolting.

CHAPTER TEN

Work on the Lunge and Long Reins

THOROUGH WORK on the lunge is of fundamental importance, for it supports the horse's training in every respect. Furnished up horses (especially jumpers) as well as youngsters should be worked on the lunge — for reasons which I will explain.

First let us take the case of a young horse on the lunge. We will need a lunging rein of about eight yards in length, a cavesson and a long whip. The cavesson is not absolutely vital; a strong head collar with a thick noseband may be substituted. It is best not to use any check reins from bit to girth, but to aim at willing and free forward movement.

At first it is advisable to use an assistant to lead the young animal round the track until it understands what is expected of it, so that it becomes gently acquainted with the exercise and gains confidence in the man and in his voice, which will gradually replace the assistant as an aid.

The use of a cavesson or halter is necessary because the horse's mouth must not be interfered with; it is therefore inadvisable to buckle the lunge to the snaffle ring. It is not necessary to buy a cavesson with lots of rings and loops to truss the horse up, for the idea of the cavesson is merely to give a strong hold on which to clip the lunging rein.

When the moment has arrived when we want to teach the young horse to go into his bridle I have combined the running rein with the lunge with considerable success (*Fig. V*). I have found that both young horses and spoiled ones soon adopt the tensile attitude with swinging back and ground-covering strides. If the horse should tend to carry his head too low in the beginning it is by no means a bad fault, for we will find this low head carriage a great asset when we start building up his jumping education. It should be noted that all jumping training should be done WITHOUT the running rein.

Fig. V

In order to work with this running rein at the lunge we need only use a stable roller with a ring on top on which to fasten the ends of the reins. The great advantage of the running rein is that the horse is able to reach his neck and head forward and down without being bound to the roller in the rigid position enforced by ordinary check or side reins. Thus the horse does not feel ill at ease and develops free and natural movement as a result of unconstrained muscle play.

Any work on the lunge over cavalettis must be done WITHOUT any running or side reins as the horse must be entirely free; besides this, the trainer should be able to see the working of the whole muscular system clearly. This exercise should preferably be done from the trot in order to increase muscle power and skill.

Particular attention must be paid to: length and evenness of stride, calmness, swing of body, skill in judging and completing the take-off, and the trajectory of the jump attaining the imagined semi-circle.

It stands to reason that the long whip should only be used to keep the horse going evenly. It should never be cracked or thrashed through the air as the whole exercise should be carried out in a quiet and fluent manner.

Work on the lunge with a "made" horse is an excellent means

of brushing up the free, swinging stride at all paces. The rider will establish a good mental contact with his horse through the use of his voice in such a way that it improves the relationship between horse and rider. For this reason it is obvious that the horse should be lunged only by those people whom the owner would allow to ride the horse, for a horse will be just as easily spoiled by bad lunging as he will by bad riding.

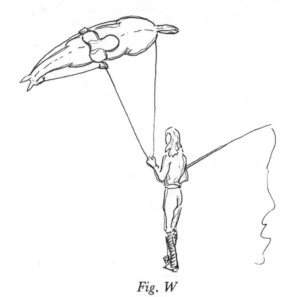

Fig. W

WORK ON THE LONG REINS

Once the young horse has learned the rudiments of lunging, better and quicker results will be obtained by the use of long reins.

The advantages of long reining are manifold, for every school movement can be taught without the disadvantage, particularly in the case of the young horse, of the rider's weight. The muscles on each side of the body may be developed equally without strain on tendons and ligaments, and the tensile attitude will readily be adopted. The trainer gains control of the hind-quarters, being able, by use of the outside rein, to prevent any tendency to swing outwards. He has the added advantage of being able to stop or shorten any gait, which is practically impossible to achieve on the lunge.

In order to start work on the long reins we will require a second lunging rein to be buckled to the other side of the cavesson noseband. The stirrup irons should be tied together under the horse's belly to prevent them from flapping, and the outside rein passed through the outside iron and round behind the horse's hocks to the instructor's hand (*Fig. W*). Care should be taken over this manœuvre as most young horses become frightened when they feel the rein flapping above their hocks when they move forward. It will be found that they soon settle down after a few circles, and work may then commence exactly the same as on the lunge.

Later on the reins may be fastened to the rings of a flexible rubber snaffle instead of to the noseband, in order to teach the horse to accept the bit and to go into his bridle — preventing him from getting behind the bit by gentle encouragement from the rein behind his hocks.

Because the trainer has control over the horse the long reins are a useful medium for correcting faults in bearing, head carriage, etc., and in reschooling spoiled or nappy horses.

Naturally work on long reins will vary according to the disposition of the individual horse. For example, a horse that sprawls along idly with nose in the air and feet dragging will need encouragement from the rein behind his hocks and from occasional taps with the whip. On the other hand the well balanced but impetuous horse will merely require a steadying hand on the reins and soothing words of encouragement. A horse is quick to respond to the trainer's voice and it is very noticeable how he reacts to a word of praise. He recognises at once by the tone of voice that he has won approval, and it acts as a psychological pat on the back.

Now let me give a few words of warning. If by any chance, as often happens, the young horse becomes frightened by the outside rein and tears panic-stricken round the enclosure it is best to drop the outside rein and pull the horse in by the inside one, speaking quietly and soothingly to him. This preliminary hazard can be overcome to a large extent by use of a fillet string attached to the saddle blanket for a few days and allowed to flap loosely above the hocks in order to accustom the pupil to the feel of the rein.

Another thing that often occurs is that the horse gives a couple of swift bucks and works the outside rein up under his tail. In this case I think the best thing to do is to keep hold of both reins and continue to give him orders to "walk" or "trot on" in confident tones as if nothing had happened. He will eventually cease his bucking and kicking and raise his tail, whereupon the rein will drop to its original position.

All this can be very frightening for both teacher and pupil the first time it happens — and I am afraid it *is* bound to happen occasionally — but do not give in and say "This horse cannot be long reined", for once he has realised that he has come to no harm he will rapidly become very sensible and quiet to handle.

For these reasons I think it is important to start work on the long reins in a small enclosure where he cannot hurt himself or his trainer, cannot escape, and where in any case he will be more inclined to work and obey commands than he would in the middle of a large open space where there are far too many distractions.

The great advantage of work on both the lunge and on the long reins is that the trainer is able to see the horse working and to note exactly what faults he is making. This is invaluable both to the inexperienced rider who simply cannot "feel" what is wrong when he is on the horse's back, and to the more expert rider who wishes to check up on the finer points.

The trainer must, however, bear in mind the fact that when the reins are attached to the snaffle rings they can exert a considerable pull on the horse's mouth, and the mouth of a young horse can easily be spoiled in this way if discretion is not used.

CONCLUSION

FINALLY I should like to say that horsemanship is vivid and alive — rigid theorems are alien to it, and the courage needed to train a horse with an open mind and an open heart is more precious than a thousand riding recipes learned parrot fashion. It is not the stringent application of complicated exercises that leads to success, but the profound study of each individual horse's psychology and physiology. The correctly trained horse must possess mental balance as well as bodily equilibrium. Patience, perseverance and consideration of physical well-being and muscular co-ordination will always lead to the winning post, but it may often be necessary to dispense with pre-conceived ideas and traditions.

When faced with a problem that cannot be answered with knowledge or from previous experience the solution will always be found in relaxation. Stop every form of compulsion, for it will only produce muscular spasms, and out of the spasm grows the rider's increasing anxiety, wrong ambition, and vanity — for which the horse must suffer.

Remember that nature does not intend to outwit, to violate, to force or to beg; the outward form produced through cunning and skill is beautiful; produced through brutality and force it is merely a trap. Due to this technical age it is too often forgotten that the horse is a living animal that cannot be bent and pressed into shape like a piece of metal in a factory.

The acme of all training is the sure skill of the horse in the open air — across country. How is the young horse to attain this skill? By education, conditioning and gymnastic training.

The horse isn't responsible for his own failure — common sense, foundation, logical build up of muscle and ability are the pathways to success.

E

APPENDIX

This appendix is an attempt to show the trainer the most important muscle groups in positive and negative function. Besides the muscles marked in the illustrations there are, of course, numerous other muscles which play their part, but in order to stress the point only the most important muscles are illustrated.

In order to make myself clear I have restricted myself to only three colours in order to show at a glance whether the case concerned deals with a *positive* muscle action or a *negative* one, that is to say, with a desirable or an undesirable effect. Mark two colours, blue and yellow as positive (desired) effects and one colour, red, as negative (undesirable) effects.

Please note that blue marked muscles are in *positive activity*, yellow marked muscles or tendons in *positive extension* in a tether-like manner, and red marked muscles are in a *negative active tension*.

This appendix should not be treated as a textbook on anatomy but as a guide for the serious horseman. I hope it will help to sharpen the eye to observe correct muscular development in the horse.

Muscle is the red meat which we find in steaks and sirloins. It consists of tissues which, when activated by a nervous impulse contract in length. Each block of this tissue is connected by ligaments to the bones. Ligaments are the stringy gristle which the butcher normally removes. Contraction in length of the muscles causes movement of the bones and thus all the horse's physical movement.

A tendon is a ligament which transfers muscular efforts along a series of bones, *i.e.*, back tendons of legs.

Muscular contractions are caused by the action of the nerves. These are divided into two kinds, sensory nerves and motor nerves.

The sensory nerves are sensitive to touch or pressure all over the horse's skin and also to heat and cold. In combination with the eyes, nose, ears and mouth they are sensitive to light, smell, sound and taste. The ends of these nerves have sensitive cells called epitheliens. These translate the outside effect into a nervous impulse which follows a system of paths via the spinal cord to the brain, which reacts by sending a variety of instructions to motor nerves, which convey them to various internal organs and the muscles. This describes what happens when the horse receives an instruction from its rider in the form of leg pressure, and consciously begins to move. But not every action that the horse makes is motivated by intelligence. Some are direct reflexes over which its brain has no control. Many, particularly those connected with discomfort, cause intense excitement and violent movement, which in itself provokes mental excitement that can be seen in the self-induced hysteria of the persistent runaway.

It is fundamental that mental tension or relaxation tends to produce a physical counterpart. I believe that the chief axiom of training the horse should be directed at influencing its intelligence to carry out its rider's demands.

MUSCLE PLATE (above)

1. Ligamentum nuchae and 1¹ lig. nucho dorsale.
2. m. semispinalis capitis.
3. m. splenius.
4. m. spinalis.
5. m. longissimus cervicis.
   (2 and 4 are the dorsal division of the longissimus dorsi 15/16).
6. m. brachiocephalicus.
7. m. serratus ventralis cervicis.
8. m. scalenus primae costae.
9. Triceps m. anconaei.
10. Biceps brachii.
10¹. Extensor m. of the knee, lacertus fibrosus.
11. Superficial flexor tendon, flexor digitalis superficialis.
11¹. Caput tendineum.
12. Deep flexor tendon, flexor digitalis profundus.

12¹. Caput tendineum.
13. Lig. sesamoidea obliqua (the suspensory ligament).
14. Main extensor, extensor digitalis comunis.
15 and 16. m. longissimus dorsi and multifidus dorsi et lumborum (connected with 2 and 4).
17. m. latissimus dorsi.
18. m. obliquus abdominis externus.
19. m. pectoralis humeri ascendens.
20. m. rectus abdominis.
21. Gluteal muscles, m. glutaeus medius.
22. Extensors of stifle joint, m. quadriceps femoris.
23. m. biceps femoris.
24. m. semitendinosus.
25. Superficial flexor tendon, flexor digitalis pedis superficialis.
26. Flexor mettatarsi (tendo femorotarseus).

68

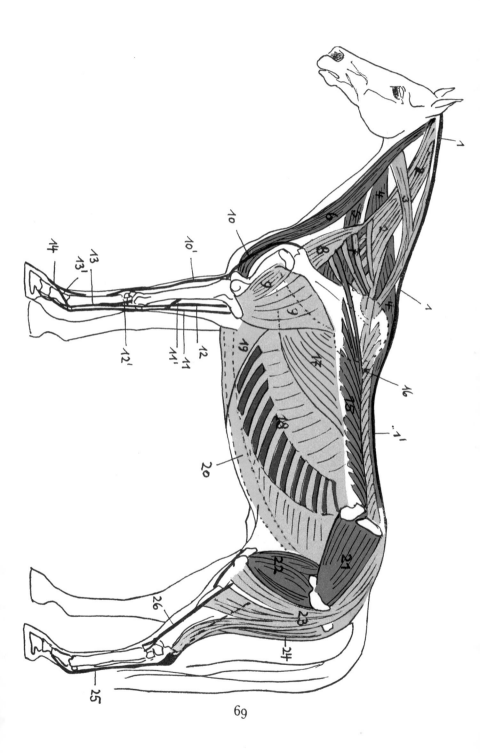

Fig. 1

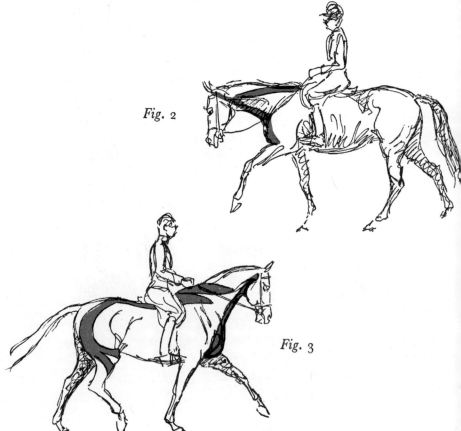

Fig. 2

Fig. 3

Fig. 4

Fig. 5

Fig. 6

Fig. 7

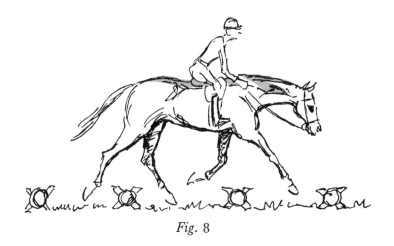

Fig. 8

Fig. 9

Fig. 10

Fig. 11

Fig. 12

Fig. 13

Fig. 14

Fig. 15

Fig. 16

Fig. 17

Fig. 18

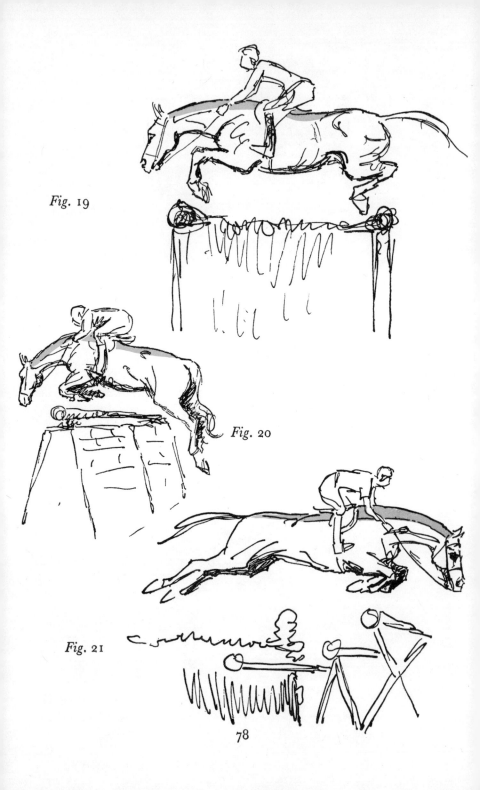

Fig. 19

Fig. 20

Fig. 21